ONCE IN VERMONT

Once in Vermont

Bob Arnold

GNOMON

I am grateful to the following editors and their presses where many of these poems first appeared in limited edition books and magazines: *Bull Head* (Joe Napora); Bull Thistle Press (Greg Joly); *The Café Review* (Steve Luttrell); Cherry Valley Editions (Charles & Pamela Plymell); Cityful Press (Darrin Daniel); *Coyote's Journal* (James Koller); *House Organ* (Kenneth Warren); *Hummingbird* (Phyllis Walsh); *Gargoyle* (Richard Peabody); *Gate* (Stefan Hyner); Longhouse (Susan Arnold); Milkweed Editions (Laure-Anne Bosselaar); *Mungo vs. Ranger* (Roger Snell); Origin Press (Cid Corman); Pentagram (Michael Tarachow); *Porch* (James Cervantes); *Potlatxch* (David Raffeld); *Shadowplay* (Jan Bender); *Shearsman* (Tony Frazer); Stingy Artist Press, U.K. (Bernard Hemensley); *Smoot* (John Levy); *Tel-Let* (John Martone); and White Pine Press (Dennis Maloney).

PUBLISHED BY
GNOMON PRESS,
P.O. BOX 475
FRANKFORT,
KY 40602-0475

for Susan & Carson

I can sing
While I'm walking

—Woody Guthrie

CONTENTS

FIRST LIGHT

ASK ME FIRST

DARLING COMPANION

LEARNED IN THE WOODS

FIRST LIGHT

SUN UP

I get up with
The birds who
Get up with me

SHOW ME

I don't walk this
Early morning, frost
On the mowing, but you do —
And when you return
I'm sitting by the
Cookstove warm as you bend
To shiver my neck a kiss —
Show me what I missed

BOW

Please don't take it
For granted this first

Light on the hillside
Bare crop ledges and

A little fresh snow —
Some mornings there I

Would warm myself before
Cutting wood, listen to

Blue jays cry someone was
About and they wanted

You to know the someone
Was you standing in the

Woods warming freely and
It could go on forever

EGG

Morning light of falling snow
We went outside and did our work
Shoveled out dog huts
Opened a trail to the chicken shed
Busted ice from water buckets

I was sweeping off long metal sheets
Over the woodpile when you said
— *see how this feels* — and in your
Gloved hand you held the flesh of
A warm egg to my icy cheek

TRAIL

I stepped off
The road onto
A trail into
Woods of
Fresh snow —
Not too deep —
Followed for
A quarter mile,
Ducking branches,
Watching them
Persist in a
Straight line
Until they went
One way, and I
The other — the
Small hand prints
Of raccoon

HERMIT

I'm the one who stacked
This stove wood ten cords
Deep under the roof of a
Broad woodshed, and sawed
Old pine boards across
To make a dutch door for
Its entry, and now I enjoy
How daylight squints into this
Burrow where round logs are
Pulled down to split each day

If you like you can find me
Talking to myself busting apart
Ash sticks with a favorite
Hatchet, its head weight just
Right, filling a kitchen basket —

Nothing like a simple tool that works

And when slipping the clear ribs
Of a whole snakeskin out of
Soft curled bark of yellow birch
I remember that tree cut down
But this visitor I missed

WOODS WORK

At lunch break unwrap
And sit in place melted
Ice never tasted better
Snow falls in big flakes
Doesn't amount to much
On hot chain saw engine

BACK TRACK

Bobcat tracks in
Wet snow behind the
House this late March —
Came back two months later
With no warning

Both wings on
One of our ducks
Spread open floating
Along the pond edge

— a good time to see
Bright under feathers
Of blue & gray/green —

But the head ripped off

BEAUTY

Traveling by car
On the interstate
North, along with many
Others, the beauty
Of the day is a farmer
And his team of work
Horses — across the median
And the other highway —
Gallantly plowing a field,
And neither seeing or
Caring if we see how good
Some of us still live

GRAIN

Two farm boys hike
Into a high pasture
Lit by rain clouds,
Scaled of singing birds,
And call out the names or
Favorite expressions of the
Dozen cows grazing who stomp
At a run uphill where
Boys and cows gather
In a circle of affection —
Tails twitching, hands slapping
Hide — all heads spilled to
A scattered pail of grain

CAN YOU IMAGINE

Can you imagine this
Being your life at six
Years old walking out
The woodshed door as
A blue heron lifts up
From our old truck
And you run inside
Even though you
May be late for
School to tell us
About the bird this
Big (arms can't spread
Yet *big* enough) as
We look into your
Expression loving that
Bird we missed

A GIFT FOR THE LIVING

We heard them —
But it was a moment
Before we saw them
Clear the trees —

I counted 66 or more
And he was still

Counting, his hand
To the sun, as
Geese flew over

IS IT

river
flowing
beneath
the stars

or stars
flowing
over the
river

GOSHAWK

4-foot wing span
Opens above me
Calls nothing
Flies over the river
Almost hides itself
Into a dead elm tree
And I stand in place watching

Solitary, the books say —

In 200 yards I'm standing
Across from the bird
And it hates it —
Quick screech calls
Fly backwards
200 yards
Lands where it began

A TREE FULL OF BIRDS

for Janine Pommy Vega

That's what I heard one morning
In a no-nothing town between
Phoenix and Tucson, where it
Appeared desolate and desperate
With a mall and motel and a big
Highway running through it all
And even the motel desk didn't
Know the name of the route number
Of the highway when I asked the
Next morning with a desire to go
To the mountains north — as if no
One went to the *mountains* from here —
But I did, and before I left, hours
Before I asked any questions, birds
By the hundreds came to the trees and
Bushes of this motel square, dipping
Even into the swimming pool, and whether
It was sunrise that lit each bird yellow
Or if in fact they were yellow and each
Singing magnificently in the coolness of
Daybreak when I was awakened gladly
And stepped out my door and onto a long
Balcony to see and hear and feel the most
Beautiful day in the world begin

ASK ME FIRST

REPUTATION

Fist-size Harley-
Davidson belt buckle he slouched
In steady rain shoveling
Snow around his truck

Parked by a driveway I shovel
As caretaker. He told me his
Life story how things hadn't
Worked out right when his family

Moved to the woods, hiking
Deep snow to a trailer
Across the river after a
Makeshift footbridge washed

Away — and by the way, long hair
In his eyes — could he cross our
Land down river where most of the
New lumber to his bridge was salvaged —

He'd heard it was best to ask me first.

LOCAL KILLERS

They're polite, both of them
Just killed a deer on our land.
One hunter needs to use the phone,
The other one doesn't want to retrace
Their hike through the woods
To his car. Could I drive them back?
The same place we buried our old dog
Last spring these two hunters have
Dragged an 8-point buck down the
Hill slope and gut it right there.
Of course they didn't know anything
About the dog and when I came upon
Them they stood rubber boots
In blood, guts matted on snow.
We left no sign or blood when we buried
The dog. Dropped a pine tree and buried
Her under the boughs, head at the stump.
She rotted. Now one of the young hunters
Is washing his big knife off in the brook
Running behind us. His balding head is
Ashen with sweat, sweater blood smeared —
He tags the deer with a rip into the
Rear leg, shows me where they shot it
Four times. They still don't know where
They are, so I point them to the road.

GOODBYE

It's been three years
Since we spoke with one
Another, and I sat in my
Old car with the engine running,
Window rolled open, and Everett
Squatted by the roadside in the
Dirty wet shadow of his homemade
Barn, munching on a cigarette stub
In a late afternoon rain.
He is leaving the valley. There is
A *For Sale* sign hammered into his
Front lawn above the retaining
Stone wall I built for him long ago.
I can remember how we cruised the
Back road in his dusty pickup truck
Robbing the walls that nobody seemed
To own because no one was around.
All that has changed.
Everyone owns land in this
Valley — now a dog and home are
Every 1000 feet — the same
Road I once followed the
Dragged trail of a porcupine
Today I wave to six new neighbors.

Everett still hasn't lost his
Handsome smile and he knows I
Think what he is thinking but
We don't say anything except we do
Need this rain as it soaks his green
Work shirt, and nearby the familiar
Drizzle from heaped manure drains
Down to the brook. That water
Once tasted like cold stone shade
And I would haul it to my cabin every
Other day — then Everett moved in and
With a farmer comes manure and in that
Pissy barn he gave me water from his tap.
No other man on this road ever gave
Me water from his tap or stood talking
In the privacy of rain or paid me one
Fall to cut his winter load of firewood
Because his back was lame and there was
Just no one else around to ask.

MANNY

The last time I saw Manny
To talk to she was
Holding two butcher
Knives in her hand
Instructing her sister-in-law
How to dress out chickens
That her brother-in-law Everett
Was slaughtering outside the barn
In the rain, with all
His young nephews watching —
The youngest shivered up
Against a barn door
With his eyes squeezed shut,
And even I knew Everett didn't
Like this job — it was all over
His face — and somehow the fresh
Whet axe felt clumsy in his hands

But not Manny — inside the barn she tossed
A scrap of plywood over a barrel
And proceeded to hold shop with
Her knives — the kids eying
The sop of guts scraped
Into a bucket — and later
They watched the dogs whine down
By the brook where this stew
Would be dumped out for them

So eight years later, this evening,
Manny drove up to our place and
Lifted herself out of the car
Telling us she was the new Avon lady —
We didn't know what to do
With that, but two hours later
Susan had bought sixteen dollars
Worth of Christmas gifts while Manny
Had told us about her past year of
A broken foot, visits to the chiropractor,
Times out here with social workers
Bringing complaints that she was again
Beating the kids — she said she
Didn't understand, and it hurt her
Because no one loved those kids
More than her — and sometimes she
Would leave here and go back to
New Hampshire where she was born
Only to find out it had
Changed for the worse —
Just like this place she was always
Turning to drive back home to

HOW IT'S DONE

Of all the things
Out in the field
Around the farm
Lee Strong might
Have taught me it
Wasn't how he used
A scythe or mid-step
Lifted its blade
To comb his stone
Regaining speed —
Though I watched all of
That — and how he
Stood in the middle
Of his work looking
At barely nothing
For a very long
Time, a match tipped
In to re-light his
Pipe — but how
Loosening a belly
Belt he privately
Let his pants drop
Those cooling
Seconds above
His knees

FARMER

There were the weeks when
We hadn't seen Everett on
The road in his truck or
In the hayfield he tended
For another landowner spreading
Lime and fertilizer, his
Mother waving to us from
Her trailer steps and we wouldn't
Bother her but went to Everett's
House back off in the woods
Knocking a few times in the
Mid-afternoon. He came to the
Door unrecognized — no cap,
A white undershirt out over
Green work trousers, mouth parting
New whiskers saying come inside.
July and curtains closed.

We sat at a table in the middle
Of one big room,
Darkness piled against
The walls, his wife at work in
Town and the kids off somewhere.
Clearing newspapers from the table
I then saw his hand and three
Fingers chopped off at the large

Knuckle, skin rounded over
For stubs. Everett held up the
Hand and said he'd been out of
Work since the accident haying.
Poured himself more coffee from
A thermos, face pale as smoke.
Shaking his head at how he wanted
To grab back the fingers in the
Baler, but the fingers were gone.

Fifteen years later I heard about
His heart attack, how he sat
Healing beside a window in his
New house near the road drinking
Coffee and reading newspapers with
Eyeglasses he never wanted anyone
To see, waving to all the neighbors
Driving by with that damaged
Hand that went back to work.

SO LONG

They had the big
Auction this morning
Up at Bud's farm. We
Saw road signs announcing
The event a week earlier and
Wondered where it was,
Coming to the news Bud
Had died last winter in his
Farmhouse, left alone those
30 years after his wife
Took her life. That was a
Long time ago — Bud hayed
His mowing 80 times since
Then — had six different dogs
All named Duke, never painted
The barn and didn't mean to
Change his living even with
The county road dividing his
House from the farm, and every
Year the cars passed faster,
The town got closer and Bud
Crossed the road not looking
Either way, the place was his.

Today old Ford out-of-state
Farm trucks with trailers
Were seen in the village
Riding up the hill to Bud's
Where his machinery and tools
Have been tagged and specialized.
The house will be sold next.
Wife, dogs, barn cats, swallows,
Straw rats, a few dusty chickens
All dead and not for sale, and
Bud made sure no one got Bud.

ONCE IN VERMONT

By the clamor and sounds
One could imagine there was
A mob of trucks and other
Vehicles pulled into the
Farmyard, but it wasn't at all
That way when I got there.
This was a long time ago.
To the life of an old-timer
Or the valley and river itself
Running through, it was only
As old as yesterday.
But I was young and so was
The teenage boy, and his father
Clayton was living down
There alone with the boy after
His wife moved out and only
A few years more before
Clayton was also gone with
A new wife and the boy would
Be old enough to marry — and
Come to think of it — I would
Around then be married, too.

It was a Saturday morning,
Clear sky open autumn day,
Trees shaken of leaves
Except for the oaks on
Owl's Head Mountain
Which always held its leaves
Into deer hunting season.
I was a friend with Clayton and
His son, or at least they were
My friends since I was a newcomer
To the valley and didn't at all
Mind helping out with their farm
Chores… walking right off the road
If they were haying, spending an
Afternoon stacking clumsy bales onto
A flat wagon and later throwing its
Load up into the barn loft hatch.
Everything built from scrap, cut
Trees for timber, salvaged shingles
And boards saved from carpentry
Jobs to finish their own house —
Pay was enough to eat,
Buy gas, keep things running.

It was the double shotgun blast
That made me curious to visit.
Both shots brilliant and decided
At ten in the morning — no way to hide it —
No one down here really to hear it.
I walked the gravel driveway between
Upper mowings before it dipped
Into the farm door yard and for all
Gun play and engine commotion
It took a moment to find where
It was coming from. Off
To one corner of the field, in
Shade of the pole barn and a few
Dead hardwood trees I caught sight
Of father and son bending down
In swift work to the far side of
A small tractor. And then one
More shotgun blast. Surrounding
All meaning of sound, making me
A little edgy if it wasn't too late
To back step away and forget what it
Was I had no idea...

And that's what took me further.
The boy saw me first, glancing
To his father who casually
Raised his head and nodded up
Hello. By then I was to the
Tractor... saw the luster of
Blood on their leg trousers and
Boots, rifle leaned against
The pitted tire, chain saw
Streaked in blood and sticky dirt,
The six and maybe I counted seven
Legs of cows, innards in a pile,
The unforgettable sensation of being
Bathed in the living, and surprised
At not suffocating in this unexpected
Horror — I mean the river is
Startling beautiful 50 feet away,
Yet there is a glory all its own
Right here — making food. It's uncouth,
Rotten, the rifle much too big for
The business, but there is
No mistake of the shot.

I would stay long enough for one last
Leg sawn off the trunk body
Later carved open and emptied —
Two cow heads rolled off into
Tall grass like the burled
Elm stumps that won't split, but those
Heads have faces looking worse dumbfounded.
The pack of mother dog and puppies
Roost in them for days.
It's just food for winter and
What happens. Next weekend
Clayton and his son might tear down
The tractor or rig the plow
On the jeep made ready
For first snow. Finally haul
Down firewood from the hills.
I came by for a short visit
And got one. Knew the job
Was done when Clayton took
Out his pipe and re-lit the
Bowl, breathing peacefully
Over his work.

FAMILY FIRE

Almost hunting season
Last week of October
No one was around when the new house
Somehow turned to fire and after
A year building for this farm family
Fell into ashes in a half hour.
The first person to get
There before the fire department
Spoke of gas tanks blowing off,
Windows melting flames,
A big blue spruce close by shredded brown.

Now down in the dungeon of the cellar
Snow shovels and pitchforks sift through
Savings of four sons, a man and woman —
Blackened chain saw bar, lost book pages,
Bills and receipts, iron coat hooks, an axe head.
No clue to the favorite family photographs
Or pet parakeet, only the twisted
Hunk of his wire cage.

I can just imagine the fright
In the bird at first sense of fire —
A quarter mile away one of our dogs
Broke the clasp to his chain
Smelling five cords of firewood
Burn all at once.

THE WALKER

Everyone who has been around
The last twenty years, at least,
Has a different story to
Remember about the Henry boy
Who walked the roads.
He's dead now.
One night after not seeing him
For a few years I came across
His tiny obituary in the newspaper
And if you hadn't known him
The notice said nothing —
Only that he lived,
Had relatives in town,
And now he was dead —
No mention that he walked
Twenty-five miles sometimes in one day.
Started off at his parents' farm and
Followed over the hill then
Tracked down into the village,
Poked through the covered bridge,
And turned on his heel to the left
Wandering down the river road —
Where two miles later he would
Pass me digging up stone for
One of the old walls around here.

Usually he was surprised when
I said hello, squinted over at
Me and raised his whole arm
In a salute, while still marching.
No one would have kept up with
His stride, and I watched him
Until he disappeared down the
Knoll — a harmless character in
Clothing that blended with the
Trees, road gravel, spring air.
Most of the people called him
Deaf, dumb or other things.
Old timers brushed his name aside
Whenever it came up, or else
Said something about "How it
Was a shame." And now as the
Town changes and funny looking
Houses are built and taxes go up
Each year for easier living
I know I miss the Henry boy,
Who I simply called the walker,
Because that's what he did
Everyday. And everyone either
Ignored him, or were used to what
They thought a pitiful sight

And no doubt he did struggle,
But this road isn't the same
Without him — it's gotten
Respectable almost — lost sight
Of one who walked these miles
For whatever his private reasons.
Nevertheless, he always saluted
His hello, passed without words.

TOM NEWALL

We haven't a clue
What he is doing —
Moving in tangle of
Thistle and goldenrod,
Grass wet to his chest,
Sun storms the barn roof —
This is Tom Newall who is
90 years old and never married,
And he might be in a habit
Of walking his fence line
Tugging off brush and tassel

My friend drives by this farm,
Always tells me the same
Story no matter how many times
As if he can't remember repeating
Why he is proud about knowing
Tom Newall — who boiled 400 gallons
Of maple syrup last year,
Triple that when he was younger —
And he never did marry, but how
Is it possible no one would fetch
This man of gentle poise and nitid
Eyes I can't forget from meeting
Him just one time

Around the house lawn trim and
Kept, chickens roost on the front
Stair stoop as if, and now
It is, perfectly normal —
There is no reason to bother
Tom Newall or any other like this
Good man — if my friend had his
Way this farmer and land and
Summit would remain as it is —
That it won't, has us look

SON OF A BITCH

The old man is a something else
Son of a bitch — no other way to
Think of it, even though it isn't
Exactly kind, but that's the way it is.
He'd bitch at you, he'd bitch at me,
Give him a topic — weather, taxes,
School budget, road maintenance, local
Politics — the first person in to see
His son at the town garage, the last person.
You knew what would be said as soon as
You left, you almost wanted it to
Begin while you were still there.
Give him time, he's heading that way.
Has helped his son at work on truck
Engines for the last twenty years and
Is now past seventy, wool capped,
Glasses, blunt forehead, all shoulders
In a sweatshirt no matter when I see
Him, even picking strawberries up on
One of the sunny hills across town, but
He is almost friendly when doing that.
A gorgeous garden, peas are always up
By early May, and he has a way and
Tenderness to work in asparagus and
Bushels of raspberries on the small
Vegetable bed he plows by the side
Of the road. Plants his bush peas

Roadside to shed dust that rises
From an overpopulated back road;
How those neighbors fly. He has bitched
And stamped so many years about the
New hoard that his language and treatment
On the subject is abbreviated to
A shake of his head — he knows you
Understand even though you weren't
Born here — the key to what it means
To be *native* in this old man's eyes,
Idiotic as it might seem since he isn't
Anymore native than the next white old
Gent still farming in town following
His own father's haul, but it does
Generate a certain policy of who-is-who
In the town. "How long you lived here?"
Is like having the last word.

The old man and his son have lived here,
Right here, no more than a few feet either
Way of birth-right, in this house and not
Including the porch where I stand trading
A few words with the old man — he tacked
That on ten years ago. We have known
One another twenty years and no matter
Each time I see him we go into the same

44

Routine of weather, seasonal news, how
Far along we both are in getting up next
Winter's wood supply. He can be counted
On to have his firewood (cut from bought logs)
Bucked and split and stacked in a half
Dozen rows thirty-two feet long fresh and
Sturdy and incredibly pleasing to the eye.
He does this all by himself with a wood splitter
And grubby chain saw, while maul and wedge
Are always close by for what won't split.
His son burns oil in a castle of a house
And can't make any sense of this wood
Infatuation but he will tell you it gives
Dad something to do, maybe keep him out
Of the garage away from the customers
Who walk away bewildered by the old man's
Statements. How in the world can one man
Be so outright angry and do such complete
Work in his garden and firewood detail?
I can picture him right now moving between
The stacks of firewood adjusting the ends
Of each row not to spill apart, raking
Bark and chips, liking every bit of the
Feeling he must have knowing it is early
May, far from winter, and here he is
Ready for anything. A son of a bitch.

BORN HERE

Mason was never meant to die —
I know we all still think that,
But he did, before winter, and
We lost one of our last town farmers.
I wonder what he would have thought
Of this past winter of nearly no snow —
Mud that we figured dry by late
March how it doubled-back after a
Week of rain ruining the roads all
Over again. Mason would have
Taken it in stride, he was born here.

How many times did he pull out
A lost visitor to the village
At the foot of his hill — door deep
Tipped in mud — shying away from
Taking money for his time as he neatly
Curled up the log chain on the rear
Tongue of his tractor. It was a half
Mile trip back up the hill. Unlike us,
Mason never had a view to the river
From his place, but he and Ruth
Often drove down the valley
Road, slow as a walk, looking into
Our yard over stone walls where Susan

Raked the wet spring flower beds,
Her hair torn in the wind.
Those were the days! If they missed
Us going down river — on the way
Back they waved — real waves, like
They meant it. We would return
The favor when hiking around the
Old woods road of Church Mountain
Rising into Mason and Ruth country,
With its hilltop view of the valley.

I always felt back at home returning
From work in the winter seeing
Distantly their row of barn windows
Lit for milking. One man and
Woman together kept the farm
Mended and able. It was one of the
Last working farms in Guilford, and
Now without Mason, there are four farms
Left. Thirty years ago, Mason always
Reminded us with his own personal
History, there were thirty farms in town.

Mason died of the old man's disease
According to Bill Weathers, who is
His cousin, and can't pronounce Alzheimer's.
When he died Ruth scrubbed every room
In the house from floor to ceiling and
Still hasn't moved Mason's old blue
Oldsmobile out of spring mud beside
The barn — which we could identify
Anywhere — even in the grocery store
Parking lot twelve miles away in town.
Ruth and Mason shopped together, cut
Hay and logs and bread together, and
Maybe it is one way for Ruth now to
Spend her own last years tending one
Cow in the barn and fattening a calf
For veal. We hiked around the mountain
Yesterday, saw the changes of a
Better road, new neighbors, and now
We scramble with our little boy
Carson who loves to run in the woods.
In all four downstairs windows of the house
Ruth's poinsettias are thriving, just
Like always — nothing has changed —
Except Mason is gone.

BAREFOOT

She'd be barefoot from
Late spring right up till
Fall and around deer season
She'd be wearing sandals.
Go down to their place —
Rusted stovepipe sticking
Out of a window, he'd be
In the small garage tooling
Under someone's car. Jump between
Mechanic work, body-shop and
Towing; most people brought
Their car there only once.
But from the mobile home steps
She'd holler another "customer"
Was calling on the telephone.
He gave me that look of importance,
Rubbed grease off his hands onto
Newspaper, trotted out of the garage.

They're both middle twenties — three kids.
The two youngest boys sit naked around a mud
Puddle, play with broken toy trucks
That look like their father's truck
— huge wheels, shattered windows.

He skips the steps up to the trailer,
Leans past her wide body with desire
Of a brother, not a husband,
Disappears for awhile.

She's eating a sandwich, I wave to her,
She smiles. Everyone who remembers her
As a teenager say she was thin, pretty,
The blonde hair always washed and combed.
This afternoon she is in a bathrobe,
Her bare feet spread thick. After she
Smiles at me she looks everywhere
Else — over the acre of junk cars,
Ratty trees, a lawn mower stuck in
High grass, down to four cows at
The furthest corner of the pasture,
Back to her two boys splashing
Like ducklings in the puddle —
Everywhere she looks, but at me.

HELLO STRANGER

His name was Carl and before he was
Even through the woodshed door coming
Into the kitchen he said, "Now what did
You do?" We've never met but I squint a
Moment closer to make sure we never have.
Carl is an electrician, I'm a carpenter,
This morning I drew a fast chopping
Blade halfway through a live-wire while
Cutting out a hatch door into the ceiling.
At first spark I stopped the sawzall. Now Carl
Is way up in the hatch fixing wire I never
Want anything to do with. It's late in the
Day, he's sweaty, punchy, clumsy for an
Electric man but it doesn't bother me
Because I like him. Did immediately.
Something about the cheap post earring
In the right ear. Something about the
Beer gut, the headband, the nonstop ramble.
Turns out he lives eight miles from where
I was born; it's been 25 years since I've
Met anyone who knows Mosserts' swimming hole
And a place called Clarksburg. "Shit, yes"

Is how Carl talks, beefy enthusiasm, as
He chips the porcelain pull switch sloppy
As ever and says he won't charge me. As if
His life has any clue about paperwork.
Let's get honest. Carl has turned 40. He
Is to be married at the end of the week
To his third wife who has two kids while
Carl has two of his own. They met at a
Country store. He bought beer and she was
The cashier. He returned every day after
Work until he gained up the nerve to ask
Her on a date. Like I said, I fell for
The guy too when he came in today walking
And talking through the woodshed door.

NEIGHBOR

They said it was a heart
Attack but it weren't no
Heart attack even though
We all seen the Rescue van
Out here and we hardly ever
Do and they pulled all three
Of his sons out of school and
Rushed them and the wife from
The Ames job real fast to the
Hospital in case it was the real
Thing but it was due to plowing
Just too much snow plowing and
Rotten weather and late nights
Riding these backwoods roads
That finally got to him just
Shy of 40 and putting on some
Extra weight and sudden like
His whole body seized up and
It must of given him a real
Scare because for a few years
Now he had turned into a regular
Son of a bitch, surly and pinched
And all cockeyed behind a beard

But since the scare and the doctor
Said take-it-easy it has been
Like when I first met him as
A boy now leaving his monster
Truck at home and walking the
Road along the river with his
Dog that he takes plowing with
Him and he waves and smiles and
The dog looks happier too

SPECIFICS

There was one stone
I set into the hut
That my neighbor Everett
Belden, a farmer, always
Remarked on liking specifically
When word of stone walls
Or such came up, "Now
There's that white rock
You did that I like," he'd
Always say and I can't
Remember if I placed it
In special or it just
Came up in the pile that
Way, but now Everett is long
Gone and the hut is 10 years
Built and so is the boy who
I made it for and whenever
The story comes up he learns
A little more about Everett,
Things gone by and the love
For something done right

DARLING
COMPANION

BABY ASLEEP

Walk around
Listening to
My boots

MOTHER & CHILD

You lift
him
with a
smile

& he
smiles

back
which lifts

you

IMMEDIATE FAMILY
for Cid

Either sentimental
Or superstitious &
Maybe both while
Finishing a day
Tree cutting I
Kneel to level
A last ash stump
Which throws up
Two wet leaves onto
The fresh wood &
Seeing that add
One more leaf be-
Tween the two
Making sure
All touch

A TRUE STORY

for Jim Koller

You'll know what I am saying
When I say
She took 4 old chickens down the road
Along the woods river
And where she let them go
A few steps into the trees
Where no one has ever lived
A porcupine, the biggest she
Had ever seen, up near
Ledge on the hillside
Close enough so they could
See each other's eyes and the
Chickens were between them
How he raised himself
How he waved to her

TEAMWORK

Every morning by the cookstove
I loop long laces on my work
Boots, tie a simple bow —
He's three years old, can't
Tie his own boots, but sits
Down next to me and unties mine

GATHERING WOOD

Dark dark in the woods
My son walks, stumbles
Over brush and limbs, looks
Where to step by watching
My legs — how I do it —
Carrying the saw, not
Much talk (he is only two)
But instead we seem to be
Singing quietly about end
Of day around us, the tall
Trees taking light, his hands
Grip dry sticks for a cookstove
And the love of his mother,
We are heading back home

APPROVAL

We hiked into the woodlot first snow
Brought home a tree for the holidays
Misshapen hemlock few would look twice at
And because you were sick we held the
Tree outside the kitchen window for
You to see, smile, nod an approval
Point quickly to a chickadee
Off on a high branch

END OF STORY

Looking out at the hillside
Across the river and over the
Trees from our home Carson asks —
"Did we climb that mountain?"
I say, "No, but mommy and I did."
Nodding, he decides, "Oh yeah,
We climbed that before I was born."

ANOTHER SIMPLE STORY

We skated and skated
Later looking over
The lake north to
Snow clouds coming

And skated some more

(you do that with a child)

And because of that
Drove home in snow

VOW

You can think there is
But there is nothing
Quite like you undressing
Me who has undressed you

THREAD

Take a blanket of red wool
Fold it into a cushion square
Beside flames of the wood fire
Where lamplight of the room
Falls the best, and right there
In the heat, away from winter
With your loom of sanded birch
I'll watch you weave the moon
Stars, river and mountains
From a trail we're on of thread

TREASURE

it's snow
falling

into her
hair

pail of
grain

pinning
onto a

heavy
wool

shirt
walking

back from
the hen

house
eggs

inside her
mittens

EVEN INSIDE

You were asleep
I blew out the lamp
Turned to you —
A firefly blinked

SUMMER LEAVES

I listen
To all

Its length
Of a tall

Maple tree
In the rain

DUO

The same bird every night
In the same tree singing
The same song that does
The same very songful
Thing inside of me

IT IS NOW THE BIRDS SETTLE

You would walk
Upstairs to our room
In the early evening
So warm
Undress, while looking to the woods
Lie down

Hours later
I would find you this way

MARRIED LIFE

I know where
The scarves are

Earrings, love
Notes and which

Soap in which
Drawer

LEAVING FOR WORK

I could hold you
All morning like this —
Loose summer dress
In my hands, brush of
Sunburn on your shoulders,
The feel of your waist,
And a game of tip-toeing
Who is taller, as we kiss
And won't let go

WAIT

All evening
A swallow has
Swept the grassy
Farmyard for one
Shed goose
Feather to stitch
Into her nest —
It is easy enough
For me to pick
Up — but I watch
Instead, until
She has it

THAT'S HER

doing farm chores, lugging
water she hikes through a field
of wet grasses in high boots
old pants & cap, a red tee
shirt she slept in & much
earlier in bed I raised this
& kissed her kissed her

LUCKY

She is right, this woman
I love, it has been a windy
Fall. And her blonde hair slips
Apart in long strands and with
One hand she combs it away from
Her face and she is smiling. For
Lunch she eats an apple and suns
Her legs, a summer skirt raised.
She is a mother. A small boy is
Napping upstairs in the house.
When awake he will chase
Leaves that fall down from the
Sky, that's how he sees it.
He calls me daddy because I am.

When I was off at work this
Morning up river laying stone
Along the road in the village
A blonde woman and her young son
Visited me. Hands cold gripping
Wet stone, boots chalked. This
Woman carried her little boy
In her arms, his green sweater
Was like the one my son wears

His mother knitted, ah the love
Of mothers! and I gathered stone
By hand and thought of blue sky
Above, day clear as the river,
And why you must love what you do.

HEREDITARY

I kid him
& he argues
with me which
turns me to
argue with
him as he
begins to
kid me

MORE FATHER & SON QUALITY TIME

He found in the farmyard
3 clean white pilgrim goose
Feathers freshly dropped

He picked up a stick
Made a blunt arrow
Strung a bow

He taped the feathers to the arrow
Filled the bow
Aimed it at me

SHE COMES TO ME THIS WAY

In her stocking feet and the
Pleats of her skirt, the way
The blouse is plain and opened
At the sand of her throat and her
Face is burned with winter and
So happy, that it is only then I
Notice something more — a
Necklace of rawhide and soapstone
Pebble, and even closer, the etch of
Turquoise on the piece, which brings
Me to her eyes...

OFF TO SCHOOL

except for
his base-
ball hat I
could kiss
him easily

DARLING COMPANION

We've come to the end of the highway
Breathless on the Panamint Range

You in a dress all blue buttoned
Down to the knees and a

Breeze parting your sweater —
I have a photograph where

You stand in sage against
A Route 395 road sign

Pointing us either north
Or south along a high

Spring snow Sierra sky and
No possible ending to the day

FROM HIS HAND

From his hand
Awakening us

In bed, two small
Carrots brought

Out of the garden
Barely washed he

Wants us to bite
Down into what he

Terms a *surprise*
And we gamely do —

Watching his smile
At this given sweet —

Knowing five years ago
He was our surprise

SMALL DIFFERENCE

We bought
a jackknife
for our son,
his first

I thought the
blade was sharp,
you liked the
pretty handle

TWO SPOONS

It's Valentine's Day —
We are 22 years married
And share strawberry shortcake
At midday, the waitress saw
To bring two spoons

Our son comes home from
Fifth grade, says Kevin
Gave Angela a $30 bracelet
And she didn't want it — all he can
Remember is most of the class cried all day

LONG TIME TOGETHER

4 dollars I paid
For this dark scarf
Of large red roses,

And love's fortune
Is that I had you
There with me, out

On the sidewalk to
Fold it, and wear
Around your neck

BREAK AWAY

Break away from the world
Even a loving child, friends
That travel long distances
To be with us; cross the
Shallow river to a bank of
Ferns, undress while wild
Chatter of the kingfisher
Hunts the long summer water
And years between us since
We've done this — naked but
For your necklace — under
Trees, evening in the leaves,
My arms circled around you

LEARNED IN
THE WOODS

BLACK BEAR

Who carried the rain on his back
Who we haven't seen for a very long time
Who knows this
Who ran like me if I ran for my life
Who crossed the wet dirt road without a track
Who had me look over the same place twice
Who mussed the deep pool river
Who reminded me of nothing else
Who crossed the road and hit a vertical bank
Who vanished up that bank of trees and brush venetian
Who isn't easy to forget
Who isn't a riddle

LESSON

There was a weasel
In the yard for months

Then one day there was
A hawk in the yard

Only his head moved
In the tree

When the hawk was gone
The weasel was gone

GEESE

They squawk & bite
& hit & scream &
Shit in your path
& destroy & you
Chase them into the
Pond in a rage

& they float

SAP

In slush of the laundromat
Parking lot, stepping
Down out of his old truck
Rubbing a big hand across
His whiskered jaw, we
Have known one another
A few seconds as I
Load three sacks of
Clean laundry into the
Trunk while he quickly
Sizes the Dodge up and
Down, glancing at mud
High on the doors, sipping
The warm sun on his
Face and the spring
Feeling he gets that
Makes him have to say
To anyone who will listen —
Bet the trees are pissing today

WOOD FOR WATER

How come this night
You wash in a pan
A shallow draw of stream water
Spilled down from wild apples
Of the mountain, where deer
Browse, make trail
Leave droppings

Hand over hand, you may
Think of it this way, or
Water that simply flows
Spreading into a sound of peepers
Where I've entered
Truck low geared
Flushing every redwing
From trees we were to clear

Blackberries grew then
Tickling stone walls
While working in the heat, high boots
Rolled pants
Many came apart wet in my hands —
Couldn't save any, not even for you

That was a half year ago —
Now dead wood dropped, hauled, split
Chickadees perch closely, fluttering pine
There is firewood to stack dry
Someplace through winter

At night you bathe cold, cold water
Heated warm —
When you dress you forget underwear
And the thin white blouse —
Just a dress, sleeveless and red

HOW TO MAKE A DECISION

This morning very early
Thinking to catch a logger
At home and knowing full
Well he would be deer
Hunting I called anyway
And receiving his wife
On the line who was not
At all helpful or friendly
I decided to call another
Logger who was off deer
Hunting but his wife was
Forthright and clear and
Honest and I decided to
Buy logs from her man

TOUGH

Leaf hangs
To one beat-up
Sawmill log

CUP (*Remembering the Old Man*)

We watched the thunderstorm
Blow over from the west,
Darken the upper hill of
Pasture, brush away
Daylight in barn
Windows, make it awful
Dark for two-in-the-afternoon

You said, *now listen*

And because you usually
Only spoke when you had
Something to say, I did
Listen, nearly held my breath
Waiting — looking up into
Your eyes and tiny white
Hairs in your nose and ears

And when the shower began
We heard it first in the
Wave of trees far off —
You looked and
Smiled at me
Hoping I had heard it —
Those few seconds in life
When earth, trees and even man
Turn their cup up to the rain

THE MAN WHO SPOKE TO ANIMALS

Today I heard Mason Weathers was put
Into the hospital a month ago after
A stroke, and I thought he was
Missing this fall when geese
Passed over his hill-farm's steel roofs
Heading south with the river.

Mason is always up and around those days
Even though he is two years retired from
Farming and is said to sit in a chair
Smoking cigarettes by his roadside window,
Wondering like a few of the old timers left —
What in the world has happened
To all this land and town he loves.

Many years ago he gave up attending
Town meeting — was busy sawing logs for taxes —
But of course it was the new people
Now in the chairs of his dead friends
That drove him away, into deeper snow
Clutching a chain saw.

One time I borrowed from Mason
His heavy snag of tractor rope
To do tree work for people he knew
In the village, and in my rush limbing
Sawed off a six foot tail of that rope.

When I brought it back Mason met me
On his porch — with its pose over the
Valley — a smile on his muscular face,
Nodded and said, "It was all right, just
Six feet shorter," then walked back inside.

They say today he has no memory for
That sort of thing. Sits up in a hospital
Bed with daily visits from his wife Ruth
Who tells friends back home Mason has
Been struck with sugar, and the stroke has
Left one side of his body blank as
A dead elm tree. Imagine a man who once
Spoke to animals ending up this way.

THE REASON I LOVE TO BUILD STONE WALLS

and have for so long
is that I need few
tools to do the job

I could walk to work
free at hand
nearly whistling

until I arrive
(not wanting to
look too happy)

and the stones
are there lopsided
appearing miserably

out of place to
someone else
as I kneel

maybe with a 3 lb.
hammer I've brought
along for company

PERFECT WORLD

I could sit here
All day trying to
Draw a circle
Perfectly round

But a bird
Made one
Into
A tree

PAL GOOSE

On that sunny day
I opened your pen door
And let you out —
You loved the sun
Sun on snow
Making tracks to the pond —
Because it got too busy
But I have no excuse how
I forgot to close your
Pen door and left home

Sometime in the evening
Faraway, thoughts to you and
The open door but I would get back
The moon was out, and you
Loved the moon —
The raccoon was out, and he
Hunts by the moon —
The next morning you were
Found dead with eyes open
Suddenly flat and huge on the snow

Too big for raccoon to even bother with
Whose blood-tracks tricky designed away
And then as if he noticed how obvious
Seemed to wash his murderous paws
Off in the snow and vanished

You were our third gander
In twenty years, flocks of
Geese once upon a time mixed
With ducks and chickens and when
Our rooster died you were the new
Rooster for the chickens —
It looked funny, it looked
Practical, you fit

I miss you now when I split
Wood and wait to hear your call
Loud and sudden and part of me

AUTOBIOGRAPHY

I stopped thinking
About my name today
When in the truck
Returning home with
My son after working
Together at a farm
Splitting wood,
Picking kindling
Around the chopping
Stump, slinging manure
Onto the winter garden
And later hiking
High into the heather
Pasture, now in the
Truck with his gloves
Still on he sized it
Up by saying he didn't
Like the name *Bob* — it
Was too short, only three
Letters — and it sounded
Like a name half-city
Half-country

SUNSHINE

in the garden
along the rows

on her long hair
down her arms

FARM HAND
for Ted Enslin

FARM HAND
climbed
a tall ladder
with hammer
pocket of
nails two
boards sawn
with a dull
bow saw now
climbs to a
high corner
of the barn
where an old
window lost
long ago of
any glass &
if people
were not
around no
one would
mind this
pigeon that
flies in this
pigeon that
flies out

first 10 years
they told you

second 10 years
they asked you

today scythed the swale
mowed the lawn
lifted the wide barn door
back onto its track
raked bark for kindling
added topsoil turning compost
took on the job to wash all
windows in the big house
looked for grapes under
frosty palm-size leaves
showed the owner how
to hang a birdfeeder

was asked
to build a
footbridge

but really
it was having
to lug by hand

down the steep
pasture & where
there was to ford

a spring runoff
two heavy planks
settled in

for them
all to
walk over

very good
money is
what pays you

& when the
youngest
daughter

living away
from home
took her

life very
good money
didn't help

heard of
the death
while using a
rake & having
to hold it off
as the father
approached un-
expectedly hugged
you in sobs

you finally
know the folks

when you've
twenty years

grown their
potatoes

everyone is the same —
first week of October
no one talks about anything
but firewood

where a
scythe
is used
always
think of
them walking
through

in Spring
the axe laid
down on
barn beam
finished at
splitting for
the season is
picked up right
there in Fall

dug the grave
when their
favorite
cat died
by his favorite
apple tree

flowers
they once
taught you

now you remind
them of their
names

the large
red barn
house-attached
has never been
painted since
you've been here

many years
now have
passed

they walk
out to
greet you

This book has been set in Robert Slimbach's

Minion & Poetica types, printed & bound

by Thomson-Shore, Inc. in an edition

of a thousand copies.

12 - 18

DATE DUE

JAN 3 20

BRODART, CO.   Cat. No. 23-221